Kid's Guide to Bugs
Children's Science & Nature

BABY PROFESSOR
EDUCATION KIDS

Speedy Publishing LLC
40 E. Main St. #1156
Newark, DE 19711
www.speedypublishing.com
Copyright 2016

Bugs are one order of insects. There are many kinds of bugs, but all of them have mouth parts that are made for piercing and sucking.

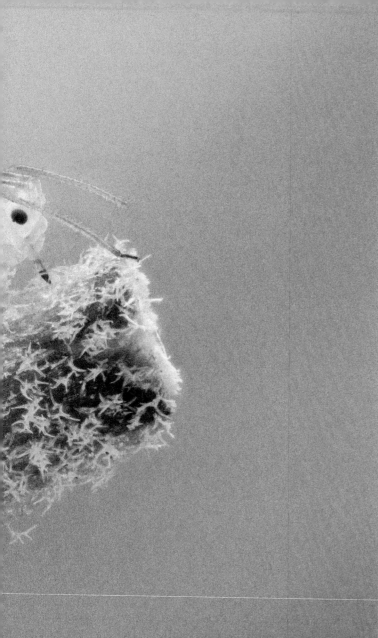

The difference between bugs and insects: The word bug is often mistakenly used to mean any small creature with legs, including most insects and other animals that are not insects, like centipedes and spiders.

A true bug is a kind of insect that has a mouth shaped like a straw. Most true bugs, such as aphids and spittlebugs, use that tough mouth part to pierce plants and drink the plant's sap or other juices.

The major difference between true bugs and other insects is their mouth parts. True bugs have specialized mouth parts that look like a long beak. These work much like a straw to suck juices. That is how food moves from the source to their mouth.

For instance, a plant-feeding true bug pierces the parts of a plant such as the stem, leaf, or other plant part using its beak and then sucks the plant juices up the food channel. Most bugs feed on certain kinds of plants and they suck fluids from those plants. However, there are some true bugs that feed on animals, like the bed bugs. There are also some bugs that feed on algae and fungi.

Bugs like the water striders and some shield bugs eat a variety of spiders, insects, and even small animals.

We can say that all true bugs are insects, but not all insects are considered true bugs—much like the phrase that all ants are insects but not all of the insects are ants.

True bugs include insects such as water bugs, stink bugs, cicadas, leafhoppers, bed bugs, and aphids. They resemble other insects in having segmented bodies, an exoskeleton, and six legs.

However, when true bugs reproduce they all hatch from their eggs as a miniature version of the adult bugs. Their front wings are thickened and are colored near where they are attached to the insect's body, but are thinner and clearer towards the hind end of the wing.

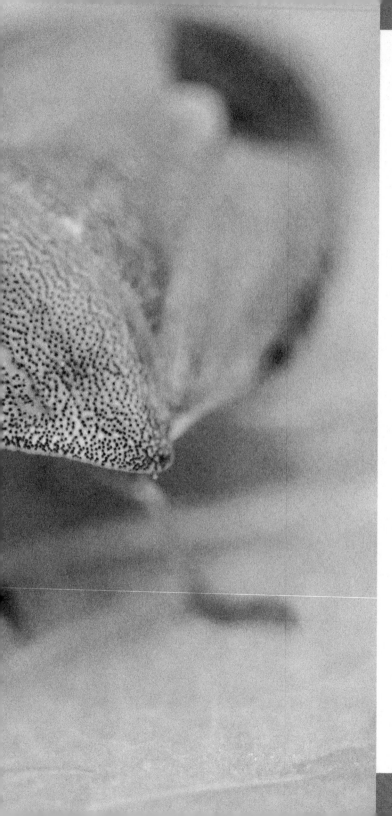

Facts about bugs: Bugs do not have lungs. Most bugs have compound eyes. Bugs are cold-blooded. Bugs are the only group among the invertebrates that have developed wings for flight. Bugs are useful because they produce silk, wax, honey and other products. They pollinate flowers and crops.

However, some bugs are considered a problem to farmers because they destroy crops. There are also bugs that carry diseases and are considered a major pest to people and animals.

What is the life cycle of bugs?

True bugs belong to the order Hemiptera. As they develop they go through three stages: egg, nymph and adult.

Before becoming adults, nymphs molt several times.

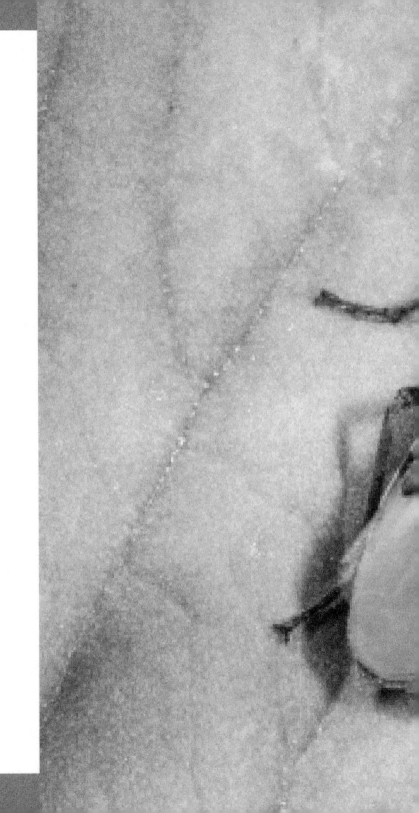

Bugs are often confused with beetles. The beetles belong to the order Coleoptera and they undergo a four-stage development: egg, larva, pupa and adult.

True bugs are part of the same order as aphids, grasshoppers and cicadas. The term Hemiptera refers to the structure of the upper wings. These wings typically have a leathery basal part and the rest of the wing is membranous.

The wings lie flat over the body with crossed wingtips when they are at rest. The scutellum or the triangular portion of the thorax which lies exposed between the wings is usually prominent.

There are about 82,000 identified species of true bugs while there are 390,000 species of beetles. Bugs are found all over the world in various habitats. Bugs are the only group of insects that has oceanic species.

Bugs include a number of pests, like squash bugs, bed bugs, stink bugs and other types like assassin bugs that feed on other insects. These assassin bugs actually benefit people by providing some pest control.

Did you enjoy reading this book? Share this to your friends.

Visit

BABY PROFESSOR
EDUCATION KIDS

www.BabyProfessorBooks.com

to download Free Baby Professor eBooks
and view our catalog of new and exciting
Children's Books

CPSIA information can be obtained
at www.ICGtesting.com
Printed in the USA
LVOW02s1550010517
532855LV00005B/122/P